Racing the Clock

Justin —
all the best — Howdeennd
Milliner

ISBN 0 340 63637 8

Printed and bound in Great Britain by Cox and Wyman Ltd,
Reading, Berkshire

Hodder Children's Books
A division of Hodder Headline plc
338 Euston Road
London NW1 3BH

Racing the Clock

Dave Morris

Hodder
Children's
Books

Introduction

This is a REBOOT adventure gamebook. A gamebook gives you the chance to decide how the story will go. You start at page 1 just as you would with a normal book - but you can enjoy a gamebook over and over again, with a different adventure each time.

You will need a die. Also have a pencil to hand, to record access codes, Delays and Game stars on the adventure notes pages at the back of the book. Access codes appear when you have discovered a useful item or clue; they show you are on the right track. Delays will affect your chances of winning your race against the clock. If you are caught up playing in a Game Cube, Game stars will tell you how well you did.

◆

Okay, that's all you need to know. Now
▶ access page 1 - and good luck!

1

Enzo has set up in business. Signs saying 'Enzo's Overwrite Delivery Service' all point to a booth at the back of Dot's Diner where Enzo is sitting, waiting for his first call. He has high hopes of being as successful as his sister one day, but he is beginning to realise that building up a business isn't that easy.

"How's the delivery service coming along?" asks Dot as she goes past with Bob.

Enzo tries to put on a brave face. "Just fine! We're talking high density here."

"Glad to hear it," says Bob. "If you need us, we'll be downstairs tracking a Tear that showed up after the last Game."

Once they're gone, Enzo's shoulders slump in disappointment. He stares gloomily at the blank vid-windows in front of him. "If I could only get one call, just to get started..."

If you think Enzo should wait patiently for someone to call, ▶access page 19. If you think he ought to swallow his pride and see if Bob and Dot can suggest anything, ▶access page 10.

Enzo finds what seems to be an elevator. It has a rusty, graffiti-covered door which opens straight onto the street. He steps inside gingerly. All the buttons are for the basement level and below - Enzo can only go down.

There is a message spray-painted onto the inside of the elevator door:

2+2=?

"That's really low density!" snorts Enzo. "But why would anyone set such an easy question? Maybe there's a catch..."

Enzo knows that Hexadecimal - a chaos virus - is never predictable. How should he answer the sum? Should Enzo press the button marked 4 (▶access page 40) or press several buttons at random (▶access page 63)?

3

"Bob's going to be deleted!" blurts out Enzo. "It's all my fault! That parcel from Megabyte was supposed to off-line Hexadecimal but somehow she found out and stuck it on Bob's face and shot him over to Silicon Tor, and now - "

"Enzo," says Dot firmly, "nothing was ever accomplished by losing your cool. Compile up. We're going to find Bob and save him. Trust me."

As they fly across the city looking for Bob, the sky suddenly goes black and is shot through with printed circuit patterns. "Warning," announces a voice, "incoming Game."

Should they try to get inside the Game before it starts (▶access page 21), or should they fly over to Silicon Tor and search for Bob (▶access page 30)?

4

As soon as Bob steps through the door he is grabbed by Hack and Slash, Megabyte's two dim-witted henchmen. "Hey! Let me go!" he yells, angrily.

"Sorry, can't hear you," says either Slash or Hack.

"Megabyte disconnected..."

"...We can't hear you because he disconnected our..."

"...our hearing circuits, so..."

They stare at one another. "Are you talking? 'Cause I'm talking!" says one.

"I reckon we're both talking," says the other.

What should Bob do? Should he try to fight them (▶access page 13), hand them the parcel (▶access page 22), or try to leave (▶access page 31)?

5

Dot is in the basement of the diner, still checking around in case there are any Tears they failed to spot earlier. When Bob hands her the parcel, she just rips it open and takes out the item inside. It is a white mask, just like those Hexadecimal wears, with a surprised expression. On its forehead is a digital counter.

"What is it?" asks Bob.

"Apart from the obvious," says Dot, "I'd guess this counter means it's some sort of bomb."

If you think Bob should use Glitch to analyse the mask, ▶access page 32. If you think he should ask Cecil who left it, ▶access page 58. If you think Phong might be able to help, ▶access page 27.

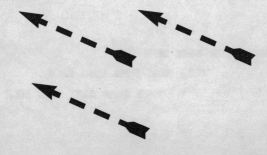

6

Bob steers between the other cars. He's in his element, completely giving in to the flow and just spinning his wheel or gunning the acceleration as his instincts tell him. Soon he's moved up into third place.

The User is way out in front, beyond a green car driven by a little binome. Suddenly the User slams on the brakes, and the green car goes into a spin, skidding out of control across the track.

What should Bob do to avoid a crash? If you think he should swerve, ▶access page 15. If you think he should hit his brakes, ▶access page 24.

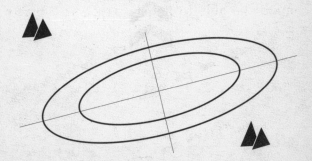

7

Bob gives a devil-may-care laugh and puts his foot down on the pedal. The mines come looming up at high speed. Bob's face is a mask of concentration. Little does he know that, on the front of his craft, another mask is steadily counting down to detonation.

Dodging the mines will be difficult at this speed. Roll a die to see how well Bob does. If you get 1-3, ▶access page 61. If you get 4-6, ▶access page 25.

The vid-window appears beside Bob's cockpit, but he flies past it so fast that it just looks like a blur. "I wonder what that was?" he says, craning his neck to look back. "Oh well, I can't worry about it now. I've got a race to win."

Watching from the ground, Dot has a worried frown. "It's no use, Enzo. By the time I got through Bob was somewhere else."

Enzo can't help gasping in admiration as he watches Bob loop the loop, but then he remembers the danger. "We'd better think of something else, sis. And fast."

Note one Delay, which will count against Enzo and Dot in their race to warn Bob about the bomb. You had better quickly think of something else for them to try. Should they drive one of the fuel trucks out across the track (▶access page 78), or try waving (▶access page 70)?

9

Time has run out, and still Bob and Enzo haven't got any idea that the parcel they're carrying is a delete bomb sent by Megabyte. As they reach the perimeter of the Game zone the bomb detonates, erasing both of them forever.

You failed to save them this time, but there's nothing to stop you having another try. Just cross out any access codes, Game stars or Delays you'd got this time, then REBOOT at **page 1**.

Bob and Dot are fixing a Tear. Enzo watches as the fizzing globe of energy drifts through the air. "Stay well back," cautions Bob. At a pulse of stabilizing radiation from Glitch, the Tear becomes a smooth sphere of silvery light. "Glitch - mend!" commands Bob. With another pulse of radiation, the stabilized Tear folds in on itself and disappears.

"Hey, Bob..." begins Enzo excitedly.

"Not now, Enzo," Dot tells him. "We have to make sure there aren't other Tears."

Enzo goes back up to the diner to find a package waiting for him. "Zat came a few nanoseconds ago," says Cecil off-handedly. "You 'ave to deliver eet to 'Exadecimal in Lost Angles."

Hexadecimal is one of the two most deadly viruses in Mainframe! Should Enzo go ahead and deliver the package (▶access page 37) or first show it to Bob and Dot (▶access page 28)?

11

Enzo finds Dot in her office at the back of the diner. She is scanning sales reports on vid-windows and making notes for her employees.

"Dot, I've got to talk to you," begins Enzo.

"Is it important?" she asks. "I'm afraid I've got a desk full of things to do right now, Enzo."

Check your list of access codes. If you have DELETE, ▶access page 3. If not, ▶access page 12.

Enzo tells his sister that he thinks Bob may be in big trouble.

"Compile up," she tells him with a smile. "I'm quite sure Bob can take care of himself. There's not much we can do that he can't."

But what Dot doesn't know is that the package Bob delivered to Hexadecimal contained a delete command. Without any warning, the command has detonated, removing all trace of Bob from Mainframe forever.

Bad luck, you didn't succeed this time. But now that you have tried once you won't make the same mistakes next time around. To have another go, cross out any access codes, Game stars and Delays that you'd picked up on this attempt, then ▶access page 1.

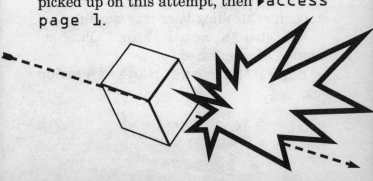

13

Hack and Slash are much stronger than Bob, but they are also slow and dim-witted. Every time they manage to grab hold of him, he twists nimbly away. On the other hand, his punches don't have much effect against their armour plating.

"Normally I'd be able to outwit them," says Bob to himself. "But Megabyte obviously thought of that - which is why he disconnected their hearing."

Finally they wrestle the parcel away from him. "We'd better take this upstairs to show the boss," they both decide.

Bob has no complaints. That was his reason for coming to Silicon Tor in the first place. He jumps back on his zipboard and streaks off into the sky.

"How did it go?" asks Dot when she meets him strolling back into the diner.

Bob gives a casual shrug. "Oh, fine. Mission accomplished."

But is it? ▶access page 14 to find out.

14

Dot has contacts all over Mainframe, so it's not long before she hears the news that's buzzing around the city. "There's been an attempt on Megabyte's life!" cries a binome who works part-time as one of Megabyte's numbers runners.

Dot looks at him with a knowing smile. "Oh yes? What happened?"

"There was a delete bomb in a package somebody delivered to him. He was lucky - it went off just before he opened it."

"Any idea who sent the parcel?" puts in Bob.

"Hack and Slash took the delivery," says the binome, shaking his head. "And they're too thick to remember who brought it."

"Well, well," says Bob. "Fancy that."

▶ access page 81.

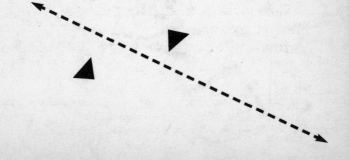

15

The green car just clips Bob's bumper before slewing across the track. It slams into the crash barrier, and hurtles end over end through the air.

Bob quickly regains control, but the green car's driver is catapaulted into the stands. Luckily the little binome has a soft landing on a pile of tyres in one of the pits.

The collision has cost Bob valuable seconds. Other cars slip past like streaks of lightning. "I'm beginning to think I'd do better on a bicycle," thinks Bob, rather annoyed with himself.

▶ access page 42.

16

Taking the mine field at low speed is Bob's best hope. Award yourself a Game star.

Other hovercraft hit the mines and disappear - leaving their startled drivers clutching their steering-wheels as they sail through the air and land with a bump by the side of the track.

Bob sets his chin and guns his hovercraft, gradually gaining on the User as they approach the end of the lap. "Okay, let's see if you can keep that lead until the end," he thinks.

▶ access page 25.

17

The gain in altitude saps some of Bob's speed, allowing the User to pull ahead into a commanding lead. Bob turns up the throttle and the sudden G-force pins him to his seat, but he still can't catch up. "I have to win!" he gasps. "There's too much at stake."

Only Enzo and Dot, who are watching anxiously from the ground, know how much is really at stake. Jumping up behind the wheel of a truck, Dot fumbles with the ignition. "We've got to get this rig started," she says to Enzo. "It's the only thing around here that's big enough to grab Bob's attention."

▶ access page 35.

18

Enzo leaves the parcel in a corner and soon forgets about it. Little does he know that it contains a delete bomb. It goes off about thirty nanoseconds later, deleting several poor binomes who had come in for a byte to eat.

"What a terrible thing to happen," says Dot, devastated by the tragedy. "Who would be so ruthless as to put a delete bomb in a package?"

Bob looks out across the city towards the baleful outline of Silicon Tor. "I can guess, but we can't prove it."

This adventure has ended in disaster, but there's nothing to stop you from having another go. Just cross out any access codes, Game stars and Delays you got this time, then REBOOT at page 1 and start again.

Note the access code ARCHIVE.

A vid-window flashes and Enzo launches into his sales pitch. "Enzo's Overwrite Delivery Service. Anyone, anywhere, anytime - " his voice falters as Megabyte's face appears in front of him.

"Enzo," says Megabyte in the friendliest of voices, "I'm thinking of using your service for all my deliveries."

Enzo can't believe what he's hearing. "Alphanumeric! You mean it?"

Megabyte touches a control on his chair and a parcel shoots out through a letter box and lands in front of Enzo. "I want you to deliver this to Hexadecimal. And Enzo, don't tell her who sent it. It's meant to be a surprise."

What should Enzo do? If he ought to tell Bob and Dot about the package, ▶access page 28. If he just ought to deliver it as agreed, ▶access page 37.

Bob is sucked down a long tunnel like a giant throat. He manages to twist in midair and lands upright on the floor of Hexadecimal's underground lair.

Hexadecimal strides forward, detaching herself from the shadows. "I was expecting a parcel, but not you." She tears off the wrapping. "A mask! How thoughtful of dear Megabyte. Tell him thanks, but I already have one."

Bob is already backing away.

"I said take it back!" she cries, pressing Megabyte's gift onto Bob's face. A moment later he is shot back up the tube to the surface.

Enzo watches Bob go flying past, high into the sky. With quick thinking he jams his zipboard into the hole in the ground, preventing it from closing completely.

▶ access page 56.

The Game Cube is coming down fast. It has already touched the upper levels of the city. As Enzo and Dot streak through the sky towards it, terrified sprites flee for their lives.

"I'm not sure if we're going to make it in time!" shouts Dot.

"We've got to," Enzo calls back. "We're Bob's only hope!"

Once the Game Cube is down, there is no way in or out until the Game is over - by which time Bob could be deleted! What's their best chance of reaching the Cube in time? Should they fly straight at it (▶access page 48), or drop down to the lowest levels and try and get in under the edge before the Cube reaches the ground (▶access page 57)?

22

"We've got orders not to accept any deliveries!" snaps Hack, thrusting the package back into Bob's hands.

"You heard what he said," says Slash, who then adds: "Even if I didn't..."

Bob can see he's not going to have any luck with these two. Megabyte has disconnected their hearing circuits so Bob can't outwit them as usual.

Bob is standing outside the building trying to think of another approach when the sky begins to grow black. He feels a familiar tingle of excitement as he looks up to see a Game Cube descending out of the flicker of an electronic storm.

Should Bob fly off towards the Game? If so, ▶access page 49. If he ought to make another attempt at getting in to see Megabyte, ▶access page 75.

23

Bob skims high over the city. Silicon Tor looms like a concrete serpent against the sky. As he approaches it, he begins to realise that returning the parcel may not be all that simple.

"If there's anything nasty inside, Megabyte won't accept it back," he thinks to himself. "And why would Megabyte send a parcel if it wasn't something nasty? So maybe my best bet would be to try something subtle instead of taking a direct approach."

Still thinking up a plan, he enters the ominous building.

▶ access page 4.

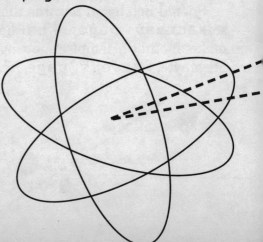

24

Bob slams down hard on the brakes. With a screech and squeal of protesting tyres, his car drops speed in time to avoid the green car, which spins off the track onto the grass verge. Bob can't resist a chuckle as he sees the driver climb out and stagger around dizzily. The poor little binome looks as if he doesn't know which way is which.

Roll a die. On a roll of 1-3, ▶access page 33. On a roll of 4 or more, ▶access page 42.

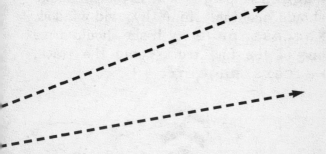

The third level of the Game turns their hovercraft into jet planes. "This is more like it!" yells Bob excitedly. "I'm right on your tail, User!"

On the ground, Enzo and Dot give up running after Bob when they see he's now airborne. "Now what?" groans Enzo. "There's got to be a way to access Bob's attention - but how?"

Dot racks her brains to think of a way. If you think she should try waving to Bob, ▶access page 70. If you think she should contact him by vid-window, ▶access page 8. If she should drive one of the fuel trucks onto the track, ▶access page 78.

The drop in altitude gives Bob a burst of speed that puts him out in front. Enzo, watching from the ground, cannot contain his excitement. Jumping up and down, he cries, "Bob's winning, sis! He's going to win!"

Dot scrambles into a truck, grabs Enzo's arm and pulls him up into the cab beside her. "Help me get this started," she says grimly, "or the only thing Bob will win is a funeral wreath."

Award yourself a Game star for quick thinking, then ▶access page 35.

27

Bob flies over to the Principle Office with the package under his arm. "Okay, Phong," he says as he saunters in. "I know the score by now. Set up a game of P.O.N.G. and, when I've trounced you, you can give me some advice about this parcel."

Phong looks up from a huge pile of print-outs and shakes his head sadly. "I'm sorry, my son. I would love a game, but I'm too busy right now."

Note that you have taken one Delay. You need to keep count of Delays; they're important when you're racing the clock.

Seeing that Phong cannot be persuaded, Bob steers his zipboard in the direction of the Gilded Gate Bridge.

▶ access page 36.

Note the access code BAUD.

Bob uses Glitch to X-ray the package. "It's a mask with a clock on the forehead..."

Enzo grabs the package back. "It's just a surprise present. I'd better get going."

Dot shakes her head. "Enzo, I can't let you go to Hexadecimal's island. It's too dangerous."

"But if I can't make my first delivery, my business is ruined before it starts!"

Dot smiles sympathetically. "Bob, will you deliver the package just this once?"

Bob reluctantly agrees - he doesn't care much for the strange floating island of Lost Angles. Do you think he should go straight to Lost Angles (▶access page 36) or drop in on Phong first (▶access page 27)?

Enzo looks around. Lost Angles gives him a headache. Streets go twisting away in impossible curves; the buildings look like fragments of a corrupted graphics program.

Enzo peers into the nearest doorway. The interior of the building is totally black. Not far off, he sees a colossal arch which seems to distort the scene behind it - it's like looking over the top of a fire.

If you think Enzo should enter the building, ▶access page 38. If he ought to fly under the arch, ▶access page 47. If he'd be better off going to fetch Dot, ▶access page 11.

There is no sign of Bob at Silicon Tor. Dot can't understand what has happened to him, but Enzo suggests Bob might have gone back to Lost Angles. "The parcel was addressed to Hexadecimal," he points out.

What do you think? Should they zip over to Lost Angles and see if Bob is there (▶access page 75) or look for someone who might have seen him (▶access page 39)?

"Hey, just a moment," says Hack - or maybe Slash.

"Hey, just a moment," says Slash - or maybe Hack.

"You can't leave without delivering that parcel," they say in unison.

Bob cunningly pretends he won't give up the parcel. "You can't have it!" he says, holding it tight.

"You can't trick us," chortles Hack. "Megabyte's disconnected our hearing circuits."

"Megabyte disconnected our hearing circuits to stop you tricking us," chimes in Slash gleefully. They grab the parcel.

"Fine," says Bob, jumping onto his zipboard. "Be seeing you."

▶ access page 14.

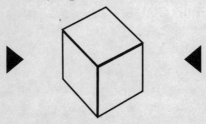

Bob scans the mask using Glitch. "It's a delete command, masked as a mask," he realises.

Enzo leans over his shoulder for a closer look. "Alphanumeric! Good thing it didn't go off while I was carrying it. Hey, Bob, look - you defused it just in time. The counter reads '1'."

"But I haven't defused it..." says Bob.

Dot has been distracted by another Tear that she's noticed drifting through the air at the back of the room. She doesn't realise the danger they're in. "Bob, I think you ought to stabilize this," she says, pointing to the Tear.

If you think Bob should deal with the Tear first of all, ▶access page 41. If he ought to grab the mask and fly out before it detonates, ▶access page 75.

Another car smashes into Bob's rear. Locked bumper to bumper, the two cars slide off the track and slam into the crash barrier. When Bob leaps out to inspect the damage, he sees at once that his car is a write-off.

The binome who was driving the other car pulls off his crash helmet. "Can't you signal when you're going to brake?" he demands.

"You ran into the back of me!" protests Bob. "You should have watched where you were going."

"Sure," snaps back the binome. "I didn't see the sign that said 'Lunatic in front'!"

Bob throws up his arms. It's not the binome he's angry with, it's himself - because that one mistake means he's out of the race.

▶ access page 80.

Dot is forced to fall back to avoid hitting the mines. She sees several other hovercraft pass her, disintegrating when they touch a mine. The drivers go sailing on through the air, apparently unharmed by the mines, which only erase the hovercraft themselves. The drivers look rather comical when they suddenly notice that their vehicles have disappeared, but Dot isn't laughing. She's too worried about Bob. "I can't see how I can possibly warn him about the bomb in time now," she thinks.

Get one Delay; you must keep a running total of these, which may be important at the end. Then ▶access page 52.

The spectators run for cover as Dot drives the fuel truck out across the track. Bob and the User are swooping down, each gaining speed as they race towards the finish line. They are now flying at an altitude of just a few metres.

"Well," says Dot, "here goes."

She turns the steering wheel round sharply, sending the truck into a skid across the track. The gleaming fuel tanks snake around, whiplashing against the crash barrier and detaching, to roll down the track like two huge silver barrels.

"Whoa!" says Bob. "Obstacle ahead. But the User mustn't win!"

What should Bob do? Bail out (▶access page 44), or try to dodge the barrels somehow (▶access page 53)?

The Gilded Gate Bridge stretches out into the space beyond Mainframe where the island-city of Lost Angles drifts. The cityscape is a barren wilderness of smooth, hot tarmac and half-ruined buildings, devoid of life. Bob cruises along on his zipboard, gradually attracting a horde of slug-like Nulls that glide along below him.

"They'd like to devour my life-energy," thinks Bob with a shudder. He looks around but cannot see any sign of a palace or tower amid the tangled debris. All the time more Nulls are collecting in the street under his zipboard. Some of them start swarming up onto chunks of masonry to try and reach him.

Should Bob keep looking for Hexadecimal's lair (▶ access page 64) or should he concentrate on getting away from the Nulls (▶ access page 55)?

Enzo glides over the Gilded Gate Bridge on his zipboard. He can't help shivering as he looks down at the blistered, twisted, insane cityscape of Lost Angles. It resembles either a war zone or a place that was left unfinished by its builders. "To think that Hexadecimal calls this 'home sweet home'!" says Enzo to himself.

He hovers lower, in the vain hope that there might be street signs. As he does, a host of glittering little slug-like creatures start to converge on the spot.

"Nulls!" says Enzo in disgust. He knows that these are the remains of sprites who were caught inside sectors that went off-line. The Nulls have only one thought: to feed off the energy of living sprites.

"I'm going to have to find Hexadecimal's lair soon," thinks Enzo. "It may be the safest place around here!"

▶ access page 64.

Enzo takes two steps into the building before he's swallowed by pitch darkness. Nervously he walks towards a tiny spark of light in the distance. As he gets closer, he gradually begins to realise what it is -

"A Null!"

Suddenly the building lights up and Enzo sees he is surrounded by hundreds of Nulls. He reacts instantly, jumping onto his zipboard and taking it straight up. He crashes through a skylight and veers back in the direction of Mainframe.

"This is too much for me to deal with on my own," he says to himself. "I'd better find Dot."

▶ access page 11.

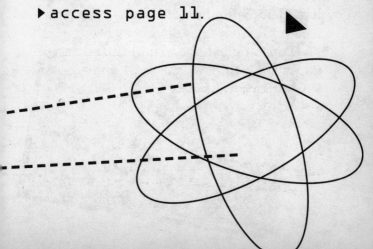

39

Dot goes up to a binome who is passing by along the street. He points to the Game Cube that is dropping out of the sky on the other side of the city. "I saw Bob grab a zipboard and fly off in the direction of that Game," he says.

"Of course," says Dot, "Bob would never pass up a Game, even at a time like this. Come on, Enzo - we've got to get there before the Game Cube touches ground."

Will they make it in time? Roll a die. If you get 1-4, ▶access page 21. If you get a 5 or 6, ▶access page 75.

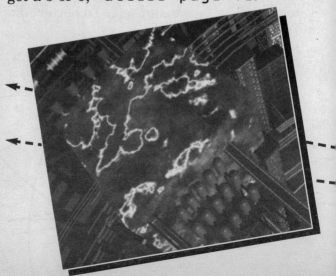

40

Wrong choice! Hexadecimal delights in distorting the laws of reality and creating chaos. In her city of Lost Angles, up isn't always the opposite of down, sometimes you can't tell left from right, and two plus two never equals four...

The moment Enzo presses the button, the floor of the elevator drops away and he is sent plunging down an infinitely long pit. His fate doesn't bear thinking about, so perhaps you would be better off having another go. Just erase any access codes, Game stars and Delays you've picked up on this attempt, then REBOOT at **page 1**.

41

Bob looks around. For less than a nanosecond he's caught in a dilemma, then he sees that the two problems have a single solution. "Glitch," he says, "stabilize that Tear into a Class One portal - "

A flickering beam of light stabs from Bob's wrist, turning the tangled ball of energy into a stable silver globe - a portal out of Mainframe into the Super Computer. With his other hand, Bob hurls the mask. It goes spinning across the room like a frisbee, shoots past Dot, and vanishes into the portal with a soft pop.

The portal shrinks and vanishes.

"Whew!" breathes Bob. "Now it'll just detonate in the Super Computer, where it can't do any real harm."

▶ access page 72.

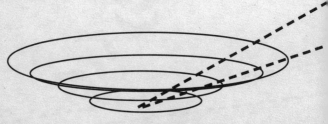

42

Bob is way behind in the race. He knows that none of the binomes have much chance of beating the User, brave as they are for trying. And, if the User wins, this whole sector of the city will go off-line - its inhabitants turned into mindless Nulls.

"I'm going to have to do something," Bob decides. "But what?"

Check your access codes. If you have EDLIN, ▶access page 51. If not, ▶access page 60.

"You take the low road," sings Dot to herself as Bob speeds ahead, "and I'll take the high road..." Pulling the wheel hard over, she flips her hovercraft right up the steep bank at the side of the track so that she sails safely over the mines.

She is catching up with Bob. Hastily she scrawls a message which she can hold up at the window for him to read: 'Get out of your car. There's a bomb.' "That ought to do the trick," she thinks, pleased with herself for coming up with such a good plan.

She is just drawing level with Bob when Enzo comes speeding up fast from behind. In his determination to warn Bob he fails to put on the brakes in time. His hovercraft crashes into the back of his sister's and both go spinning off the track.

They watch Bob go racing off into the distance. "I think we just blew our last chance," groans Enzo.

▶ access page 52 to see if he's right.

"Glitch - parachute!"

Bob jabs the eject button. The cockpit cover blows open and he's shot to safety in the nick of time. An instant later, his jet collides with the User's and both go tumbling into the fuel tanks. Bob watches them explode in a blossom of pixel-outlined flame as he drifts down to a soft landing by the side of the track.

Then there is a strange crackling sound and a blinding flash of blue light from the centre of the inferno. The flames disappear along with the wreckage as the effect of the delete bomb spreads rapidly.

"Warning," announces a disembodied voice, "Game corruption."

Bob shakes his head and stares at the swelling blue light. "Not good. This is not good..."

▶ access page 62.

The warning comes in the nick of time. Bob swings his arm around, throwing the mask like a discus. It goes sailing up through the air above the stands. The watching binomes, having overheard Dot shouting about a bomb, scurry for cover.

The mask detonates, but instead of an explosion there is a dazzling flash of blue light. The globe of light swells rapidly.

Sections of the sky drop like a broken glass skylight, and an ever-calm voice announces, "Game corruption. Warning, Game corruption."

"What's happening?" gasps Dot, as she stands staring in horror at the rapidly expanding globe of light.

"I don't know - I never saw anything like this before," says Bob. "But it's not good."

That's for sure. ▶access page 62 to see if they can get out of trouble this time.

Bob breaks away from his friends and goes charging back towards the line across the track. "I've got to finish it!" he calls over the screeching wind.

"Bob!" cries Dot in shock and surprise. "This is no time to worry about the Game!"

But in fact, Bob is worried about much more than his reputation as a Game player. He has realised that the delete bomb has caused the Game to corrupt. The world is literally breaking apart under their feet, and only by ending the Game can Bob put a stop to it...

As he crosses the finish line, the Game automatically registers a winner and closes down. The racetrack and scenery vanish. The blinding light and the wind stop, as the Game switches off. Everything is back to normal.

▶ access page 72.

Like many features of Lost Angles, the arch connects two locations that could not possibly be reached by the normal laws of reality. Enzo suddenly finds himself in the mouth of a tunnel that leads into a huge underground chamber, where Bob is talking to Hexadecimal.

"Take this mask back to Megabyte," Hexadecimal is saying.

Bob shakes his head. "I'd rather not, if you don't mind."

Hexadecimal's face flickers through a range of emotions, finally settling on a scowl. "But I do mind!"

Enzo watches in alarm as she presses the mask onto Bob's face and then, while he is struggling to pull it off, sends him shooting back up the shaft to the surface.

What should Enzo do? Should he hide, back in the shadows (▶access page 56) or run forward to help Bob (▶access page 65)?

Dot and Enzo catch a glimpse of Bob inside the affected zone, then the wall of the Cube falls like a door between them. They have to bank sharply to avoid crashing into it.

"Cursors and crashes!" cries Enzo. "We lost him."

"Maybe not," says Dot, grabbing his arm. She guides their zipboards in a full-power nose dive towards the ground, pulling up at the last moment. There is still a chance of getting in under the edge of the Game Cube before it touches down in the lowest level of the city.

Note that you have taken one Delay. You'll need to keep a running total of Delays, which will count against Dot and Enzo when it comes to warning Bob about the delete bomb.

Now roll a die. If you get 1-4, ▶access page 57. If you get 5 or 6, ▶access page 75.

49

Dot and Enzo have flown over to Silicon Tor to see how Bob got on. They are just in time to see him flying off towards the Game Cube on the other side of town.

"He didn't deliver the parcel!" says Enzo, pointing up at Bob as he recedes into the distance.

"Ssh," says Dot.

She is listening at the doorway. Inside the building, Hack and Slash are congratulating themselves on having dealt with Bob. "Little does he know that parcel's got a delete bomb inside it!" they are chortling to themselves.

"A delete bomb!" cries Dot. "We've got to warn Bob. You know what that means, Enzo?"

Enzo is already back on his zipboard. "Sure," he says excitedly. "We're going to join the Game!"

That's if they can get there in time.

▶ access page 21.

Bob screeches off down the track with the other cars in hot pursuit. Dot and Enzo are left standing in a cloud of exhaust fumes and hot rubber. But they caught a glimpse of Megabyte's delete bomb - it is lodged over the hood ornament on Bob's car.

"Bob's racing against the clock," says Dot, "and the clock's going to win. We've got to stop him, Enzo."

"Stop him?" says Enzo. "How will we even catch him?"

What do you think they should do? Should they get cars of their own and join the race (▶access page 59), or put a message for Bob on the track loudspeakers (▶access page 68)?

51

Bob floors the accelerator and manages to pull up among the slower cars, before catching sight of Dot gaining on him.

"That's funny," thinks Bob, "what's she waving for?" Nonetheless he gives Dot a cheery wave in return.

She pulls level and screams at him over the noise of the engine, "Your car's a bomb!"

"You're telling me. It comes with only one nitro boost!"

"No, Bob - look!"

Bob sees that she's pointing to the hood of his car, but he can't see the mask bomb from where he's sitting. "I think the engine's at the back of these cars, actually," he shouts back.

Dot growls under her breath. She's going to have to get his attention some other way.

▶ access page 69.

The User's hovercraft is still ahead, and it hasn't run out of mines yet. Another dozen or so pour out, right in Bob's path. He's seen what the mines did to other hovercraft that hit them - the drivers weren't hurt, only their vehicles were destroyed. But Bob can't afford to lose this race. If he does, the whole city sector will go off-line.

What do you suggest he should do? If Bob's best chance is to slow down and try and avoid the mines, ▶access page 16. If he'd be better off accelerating through them and just trusting to luck, ▶access page 7.

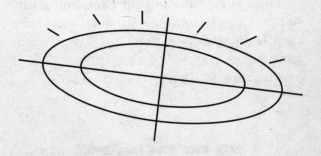

Bob pulls back on the joystick, pulling the nose of his plane up so that it just misses the rolling fuel tanks. The User isn't so lucky, colliding straight into them at full speed. Bob looks back to see a fountain of pixel-shaped flames followed an instant later by the roar of an explosion.

"Whew!" he says to himself. "I was almost blown sky high." He doesn't know that the delete bomb on the front of his plane is just nanoseconds from detonating.

Glancing down, Bob sees Dot and Enzo jump out of the truck and start waving at him. "That's strange," he thinks. "They went to a lot of trouble to access my attention. I wonder why..."

Time is running out for Bob. Roll a die, subtracting 1 from the number rolled for each Delay you've picked up. If your total score is 4 or less, ▶access page 75. If 5 or more, ▶access page 71.

54

The spreading effect of the delete bomb is affecting the Game itself, sucking scenery into the heart of a deadly data-storm.

"What happens if we get sucked in?" shouts Enzo over the roar of the wind.

Bob points to a truck that goes skidding across the track. As it touches the ball of light it disintegrates, appearing for just an instant as separate pixels like scattered window panes, before vanishing altogether.

It's impossible to move against the powerful gale sucking them back. Enzo puts his head down and grits his teeth, as the noise builds to a deafening crescendo - FWOOM! Then silence.

They look up. The blinding light, the wind and the Game itself has gone. Everything is back to normal.

▶ access page 72.

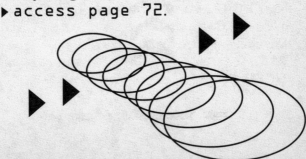

The Nulls follow Bob as far as the Gilded Gate Bridge and then stop. He hovers in the air and watches them through narrowed eyes. He is torn between common sense, which urges him back to Mainframe, and his natural desire for adventure, which makes him want to zip past the Nulls into Lost Angles.

"There's something weird going on," he decides at last. "I'd better get this package back to whoever sent it. That's the only way to get to the bottom of the mystery."

Check your access codes. If you have ARCHIVE, ▶access page 66. If not, ▶access page 67.

Note the access code DELETE.

Enzo listens in as Hexadecimal crows to her pet, Scuzzy, saying, "Bob should get to Megabyte's tower just as the clock reaches zero. I'd like to see Megabyte's face when his own delete-bomb goes off."

Enzo is horrified. "If Bob's holding that mask when it detonates," he thinks, "he'll be deleted along with Megabyte!"

Enzo leaps onto his zipboard. If you think he should go after Bob, ▶access page 74. If you think

he should go and find Dot, ▶access page 11.

57

As they run forward, Enzo and Dot can see that the area inside the Game Cube has changed to resemble a racetrack. The Game is Formula One. Bob, standing with several other sprites at the starting line, touches his chest emblem and shouts, "REBOOT!" A racing car appears and Bob climbs in. Several of the pluckier sprites follow suit. In pole position is an ominous white car with no driver at the wheel.

"The User's car," says Enzo, pointing. "That's the one Bob's got to beat."

Dot shakes her head. "For once the User isn't the big problem. If Bob isn't warned about the bomb in the mask he's carrying, he'll be deleted when it goes off."

A binome by the side of the track drops a chequered flag to signal the start of the race - and they're off!

▶ access page 50.

Bob strolls over to a table where Cecil is serving some customers. "You don't happen to know who left a parcel here for Enzo to deliver?" he asks.

Cecil throws him a haughty look. "It may have been..."

"Hey," says one of the binomes sitting at the table, "there's no bitstream in my code cola!"

"Excusez-moi, m'sieur!" cries Cecil. He flits off with the code cola and returns with a fresh one, which he places on the table with an elegant flourish.

Bob clears his throat. "You were saying, Cecil?"

"Hmm? Oh, zee parcel. Oui. I zink it was left by one of Megabyte's goons."

"Megabyte!" cries Bob, alarmed. "That can only mean trouble. I'd better zip over to Silicon Tor and find out what's going on."

Bob hops on his zipboard and streaks off into the sky. But has he left it too late? Roll a die. If you get 1-3, ▶ access page 75. If you get 3 or more, ▶ access page 23.

Dot and Enzo get in their cars and go roaring off. They are way behind, but some daring driving soon brings them up level with the pack. They can see Bob in the lead.

The User's sleek white car suddenly puts on a burst of incredible speed, shooting way out in front. Bob is amazed for a moment, then he scans the dashboard and notices a button with a flame icon next to it. "Nitro boosters," he mutters to himself. "Useful when you need that little something extra."

Several other cars have also used their nitros and are moving up past Bob. Should he press the button now (▶ access page 77), or save his own car's nitro boost for later (▶access page 6)?

60

The nitro fires, giving a burst of speed that flattens Bob back in his seat. The extra boost is all he needed to cruise past the other cars until he is up among the frontrunners. Now he's almost level with the User as they come up to the end of the first lap.

Award yourself one Game star and
▶access page 69.

61

Bob runs smack into a mine. His hovercraft vanishes, not with a bang but with a soft pop, and he goes flying through the air. Luckily the awning over the commentators' box gives him a soft landing. As he clambers down, one of the commentators thrusts a microphone under his nose and asks, "Got a message for the sports fans out there, Bob?"

"Yeah," says Bob. "Watch out for those minefields."

As he walks away, he sees the mask lying by the side of the racetrack. "Oh, it's lucky I found that," he says, picking it up. Little does he know...

▶ access page 80.

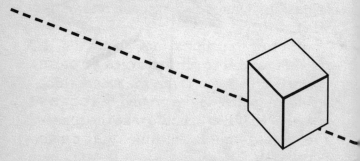

The light gives off sparks of violet radiation that open up cracks in the Game. It begins to suck things in with such force that the wind seems to scream. Cars, trees, tyres, grandstand seats - everything goes tumbling towards the centre of the light.

The binome spectators turn and run for their lives. The commentator stays at his microphone just long enough to say, "That's all we have for you today, sports fans!" and then he too flees as fast as his legs will carry him.

"Hey, I've never seen anything like that before," gasps Enzo.

"And you'll never see anything like anything again if we let ourselves get sucked in!" shouts Bob over the roar of the wind.

What do you think they should do? If the best thing is to run for cover, ▶access page 54. If you think the safest thing would be to dive to the ground, ▶access page 76. If Bob ought to take the time to run across the finish line, ▶access page 46.

63

The lift shoots down the shaft like a speck of dust into a vacuum cleaner. It stops with a jolt and the door flies open. Enzo is flung out, dizzy and frightened, on the floor of a huge underground chamber. Hexadecimal looks down from her throne like a scarlet spider in its web.

"Er... I buh-brought you a puh-package, Ms Decimal," stutters Enzo.

"I know; it's a mask," she says, not bothering to take it from him. "I've already got all the masks I need. Return to sender, if you don't mind."

With that she shoots Enzo back up to the surface. He is now at a loss to know what to do with the package. He flies back to the diner, relieved to be out of Lost Angles.

Check your access codes. If you have ARCHIVE, ▶access page 66. If not, ▶access page 18.

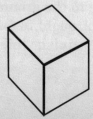

64

Meanwhile, in a secret lair deep below the surface of Lost Angles, Hexadecimal's little pet, Scuzzy, has just returned from Megabyte's tower, and is replaying what he observed there. Hexadecimal's face takes on a shocked expression as she watches the images appearing in Scuzzy's dome.

Megabyte is wrapping up a package. "A delete command is hidden in the mask. Hexadecimal will never know what erased her. Now all I need is some unsuspecting fool to deliver it. Ah, like this poor boy..."

"Try and delete me, would he?" muses Hexadecimal, laughing. "He's the one who'll be getting a surprise - when I delete first his delivery boy, then Megabyte himself!"

Check your access codes. If you have BAUD, ▶access page 73. Otherwise ▶access page 2.

65

Enzo is plucky, but there's nothing he can do against a powerful virus-queen like Hexadecimal. She shows him a face of pure contempt and sends him flying up the shaft behind Bob. Luckily Enzo has kept hold of his zipboard, and manages to fly up to where Bob is tumbling through the air. Between them they get the mask off.

"Phew," says Bob. "Thanks, Enzo."

Enzo swells up with pride at getting praise from his idol, but before he can reply there is a crackling in the sky and a familiar warning siren that makes their pulses race.

"A Game!" yells Bob excitedly as the huge block descends towards the city. "Let's get over there."

If you have the code ARCHIVE, ▸access page 79. If not, ▸access page 9.

Enzo tells Bob who sent the package. "It isn't like Megabyte to send gift-wrapped presents to Hexadecimal," says Bob. "He's not the romantic sort."

Dot takes the package from Enzo and pushes it into Bob's hands. "Bob," she says, "I think you'd better return this to Megabyte. I don't know what it is, but I'm certain it's nothing nice."

Bob flies over to Silicon Tor. As he drifts in towards that ominous structure towering above the skyline, he drops the zipboard down to street level. "I'm going to have to be clever about this," he decides. "If there's anything nasty in the parcel, Megabyte won't accept it back. And why would he send a parcel unless it had something nasty in it? So maybe a direct approach isn't my best bet."

▶ access page 4.

"There's another mystery," admits Enzo. "I don't actually know who sent the package. It was just left in my office - er, that is, at my table in the diner."

Bob gives the package a shake. "I wonder what it is. And how can we find out who sent it?"

What do you think? Who should they turn to for advice? If they should ask Cecil, the waiter, ▶access page 58. If you think Dot might have some idea, ▶access page 5.

Dot runs over to the commentators' box, grabs a microphone and shouts into it, "Bob, you've got to pull over right now. You're carrying a delete bomb!"

Her message blares out from loudspeakers all along the track, but it is no good. Bob can't hear anything over the noise of the car engine.

Note down that this has cost one Delay. You need to keep a running tally of Delays, which will be important when it comes to deciding if Dot and Enzo can warn Bob in time.

Now ▸access page 59.

The User roars past the flag with Bob in hot pursuit. As they pass the line, there is a short burst of digitized music and the Game switches to level two. Now their cars have turned into jet powered hovercraft and the track is a slalom run with steeply banked sides.

Bob is grinning to himself as he gains on the User. "Okay, you beat me to level two," he mutters under his breath, "but it's who's ahead at the end that counts."

The User might almost have read his mind because, as if in reply, a host of small black mines appear out of the back of the hovercraft. Dot sees them too, just as she is drawing level with Bob.

Let's get Dot out of trouble first. What should she do about the mines? If you think she should put her brakes on, ▶access page 34. If you think she should swerve sharply aside, ▶access page 43.

They stand in the middle of the track and wave as Bob zooms overhead.

"This is no good," says Dot. "He's going too fast to notice us. We need something that will get his attention."

"And we need it now !" agrees Enzo. "We have to warn Bob about the bomb - while there's still a Bob to warn."

The time they wasted waving means that you must note one Delay. These Delays will count against them in their race against the clock. You had better quickly think of something else for them to try. Should they drive one of the fuel trucks out across the track (▶access page 78), or try getting touch with Bob by vidwindow (▶access page 8)?

71

Bob realises that Dot and Enzo wouldn't have taken such a risk unless he was already in deadly danger. "Glitch - analysis!" he commands.

Glitch plugs into the cockpit computer and runs a diagnostic check on the jet plane. A flashing light located at the front of the plane shows up on Glitch's display.

"I've picked up a delete bomb from somewhere," says Bob in horror. "I think it's time I wasn't here."

A wise decision - but is he in time?
▶ access page 44 to find out.

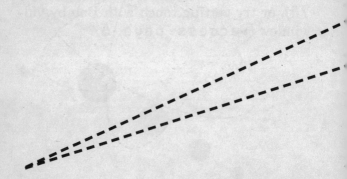

72

Now you have a chance to see how well you did during the Game. If you scored three Game stars you rate as a Champion player. If you scored two Game stars you rate as a Master. A score of one Game star means you are an Expert. If you got no stars you are only a Novice player - but all the same, you did help save Bob from being deleted!

Now ▶access page 81.

Now ▶access page 81.

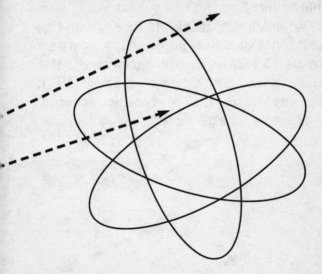

Bob is cruising along a few metres above the street. He has no time to react when the hard road surface becomes fluid and drops away, leaving a circular shaft. Bob is sucked down out of sight.

Enzo, who was following out of curiosity, is alarmed to see this. "Oh boy, the streets in Lost Angles really suck!" he gasps aloud. "Bob could be in big trouble now. What should I do?"

What do you think? If Enzo should go and tell Dot what happened, ▶access page 11. If he should wait to see if Bob surfaces again, ▶access page 20. If he ought to try a rescue attempt, ▶access page 29.

Enzo flies his zipboard over to Silicon Tor, but there is no sign of Bob. Apparently he managed to get the mask off and somehow stopped himself hurtling through the air - probably using Glitch, guesses Enzo.

The sky turns dark. Lightning like wiring on a circuit board crackles high above as a massive block of energy descends towards the city.

"A Game!" cries Enzo in delight. "Pixelacious! Bob's bound to head straight for it."

He swoops down on his zipboard in time to see Dot flying towards the Game Cube too. "Dot," he calls, "there's a delete command hidden in the mask Bob's carrying. We've got to warn him."

Make a note of one Delay for the time Enzo wasted going to Silicon Tor. You'll need to keep a running total of Delays, which are important when you're racing against the clock. When you've done that,
▶access page 57.

75

Time has run out. The delete command inside Megabyte's gift goes off, erasing Bob before he even knows what has happened.

Oh dear. Maybe you'd like to try again and see if you can do better next time? If so, cross off any access codes, Delays or Game stars you got this time, then
▶access page 1.

The light spreads rapidly - an uncontrollable and unstoppable force. Everything it touches breaks apart into ragged pixels and then is sucked into the heart of the maelstrom. Lying on the ground, Bob and the others cannot escape. They too are pulled in by the force of the wind. They suffer the same fate as the rest of the debris: within a nanosecond there is nothing left to show they were ever there.

This adventure ended in disaster, but there's nothing to stop you having another go. Just cross out any access codes, Game stars or Delays you got this time, then REBOOT at page 1.

Bob pushes the button and is pressed back in his seat as the car accelerates forward. The nitro almost doubles his speed, but the trouble is that he can't get full advantage from it while he is tightly bunched in among the other cars. By the time he's weaved his way to the front, most of the boost is used up. The User is still way ahead.

Note the access code EDLIN and then
▶access page 6.

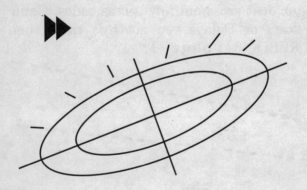

78

Exhilarated by the thrust of his jet plane, Bob actually chuckles to himself as he gains on the User. This is the kind of contest he enjoys - neck-and-neck thrills with a dash of deadly danger. Of course, he might not be enjoying it so much if he knew his plane is carrying a delete bomb that is set to go off in just a few more nanoseconds.

The User banks, following the curve in the track below. Do you think Bob should steer high (▶access page 17), or dive underneath the User's plane (▶access page 26)?

The area inside the Game Cube becomes a racetrack. "It's Formula One," says Bob with a confident grin. "REBOOT!" He touches his chest emblem and instantly a sports car appears. Bob climbs in and fastens his seat belt. Several bold sprites do the same.

Bob glances to his left at a white car with no driver - the User's car. He must beat the User to prevent this sector from being off-lined.

Dot comes rushing over to Enzo, who is trying to find the space to access a car of his own. "Where's Bob?" she gasps.

"Over there. Are you joining in the race as well?"

Dot has other things on her mind."I've run some checks on that package. You didn't tell me it's from Megabyte. I've got to warn Bob there's probably a bomb inside."

Too late. A binome drops a chequered flag and the cars roar away.

▶ access page 50.

Bob is just standing by the side of the track watching the race when Dot and Enzo come hurrying up.

"Hey, you guys," says Bob with a grin. "Great Game, isn't it?"

"Forget the Game for once," yells Dot. "That parcel you're carrying has a delete bomb inside. Get rid of it!"

But has Dot beaten the clock? Roll a die and subtract 1 from the total for each Delay you picked up. If your final score is 3 or less, ▶access page 75. If it is 4 or more, ▶access page 45.

Later, Enzo is sitting quietly in a corner of the diner when a vid-window opens in front of him. "Megabyte," he gulps. "What a surprise. What can I do for you?"

"Enzo," says Megabyte. He doesn't look pleased, and his voice is a bad-tempered growl. "I shan't be using you for my deliveries in future."

Enzo pretends to look bothered by this, but in reality he's delighted. "Oh... er, that's too bad. What a shame. Well, can't win 'em all."

The vid-window goes blank. Enzo looks up as Bob sits himself down on the other side of the table. "Don't feel bad about your business not working out," says Bob.

"Really, I don't," replies Enzo. "I've thought up a new angle, you see. Enzo's Data-match Dating Service. What do you think? Nifty idea, huh?"

Bob can only shake his head. "Oh boy..."

Access Codes

— — — — — — — — — —

DATA RECORD

Access Codes

- - - - - - - - -

DATA RECORD

Access Codes

------- -- -- -- -- -- -- --

DATA RECORD

Game Stars

DATA RECORD

Game Stars

DATA RECORD

Game Stars

DATA RECORD

Delays

DATA RECORD
Delays

- - - - - - - -

Have you read these other exciting ReBoot Adventure Game Books?

- Virtual Life

- The Knight Watchmen

- The Virus Hunter

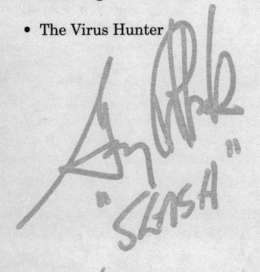